THE CHALDÆAN ORACLES OF ZOROASTER

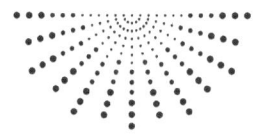

W. WYNN WESTCOTT

CONTENTS

Preface by Sapere Aude	1
Introduction by L. O.	6
THE ORACLES OF ZOROASTER	26
IDEAS	37
INTELLIGIBLES, INTELLECTUALS, IYNGES, SYNOCHES, TELETARCHÆ, FOUNTAINS, PRINCIPLES, HECATE AND DÆMONS	
PARTICULAR SOULS	46
SOUL, LIFE, MAN	
MATTER	52
THE WORLD—AND NATURE	
MAGICAL AND PHILOSOPHICAL PRECEPTS	61
ORACLES FROM PORPHYRY	73

PREFACE BY SAPERE AUDE

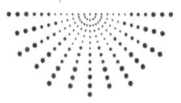

THESE Oracles are considered to embody many of the principal features of Chaldæan philosophy. They have come down to us through Greek translations and were held in the greatest esteem throughout antiquity, a sentiment which was shared alike by the early Christian Fathers and the later Platonists. The doctrines contained therein are attributed to Zoroaster, though to which particular Zoroaster is not known; historians give notices of as many as six different individuals all bearing that name, which was probably the title of the Prince of the Magi, and a generic term. The word Zoroaster is by various authorities differently derived: Kircher furnishes one of the most interesting derivations when he seeks to show that it comes from TzURA = a figure, and TzIUR= to fashion, ASH = fire, and STR = hidden; from these he gets the words Zairaster = fashioning images of hidden fire;—or Tzuraster=the image of secret things. Others derive it from Chaldee and Greek words meaning " a contemplator of the Stars."

It is not, of course, pretended that this collection as it stands is other than disjointed and fragmentary, and it is more than probable that the true sense of many passages has been obscured, and even in some cases hopelessly obliterated, by inadequate translation.

Where it has been possible to do so, an attempt has been made to elucidate doubtful or ambiguous expressions, either by modifying the existing translation from the Greek, where deemed permissible, or by appending annotations.

It has been suggested by some that these Oracles are of Greek invention, but it has already been pointed out by Stanley that Picus de Mirandula assured Ficinus that *he* had the Chaldee Original in his possession, "in which those things which are faulty and defective in the Greek are read perfect and entire," and Ficinus indeed states that he found this MS. upon the death of Mirandula. In addition to this, it should be noted that here and there in the original Greek version, words occur which are not of Greek extraction at all, but are Hellenised Chaldee.

Berosus is said to be the first who introduced the writings of the Chaldæans concerning Astronomy and Philosophy among the Greeks,[1] and it is certain that the traditions of Chaldea very largely influenced Greek thought. Taylor considers that some of these mystical utterances are the sources whence the sublime conceptions of Plato were formed, and large commentaries were written upon them by Porphyry,

Iamblichus, Proclus, Pletho and Psellus. That men of such great learning and sagacity should have thought so highly of these Oracles, is a fact which in itself should commend them to our attention.

The term "Oracles" was probably bestowed upon these epigrammatic utterances in order to enforce the idea of their profound and deeply mysterious nature. The Chaldæans, however, had an Oracle, which they venerated as highly as the Greeks did that at Delphi.[2]

We are indebted to both Psellus and Pletho, for comments at some length upon the Chaldæan Oracles, and the collection adduced by these writers has been considerably enlarged by Franciscus Patricius, who made many additions from Proclus, Hermias, Simplicius, Damascius, Synesius, Olympiodorus, Nicephorus and Arnobius; his collection, which comprised some 324 oracles under general heads, was published in Latin in 1593, and constitutes the groundwork of the later classification arrived at by Taylor and Cory; all of these editions have been utilised in producing the present revise.

A certain portion of these Oracles collected by Psellus, appear to be correctly attributed to a Chaldæan Zoroaster of very early date, and are marked "Z," following the method indicated by Taylor, with one or two exceptions. Another portion is attributed to a sect of philosophers named Theurgists, who flourished during the reign of Marcus Antoninus, upon the authority of Proclus,[3] and these are marked "T." Oracles additional to these two series and of less definite source are marked "Z or T." Other oracular passages from miscellaneous authors are indicated by their names.

The printed copies of the Oracles to be found in England are the following:—

- 1. *Oracula Magica*, Ludovicus Tiletanus, Paris, 1563.
- 2. *Zoroaster et ejus 320 oracula Chaldaica;* by Franciscus Patricius. . . . 1593.
- 3. Fred. Morellus; *Zoroastris oracula*, 1597. Supplies about a hundred verses.
- 4. Otto Heurnius; *Barbaricæ Philosophiæ antiquitatum libri duo*, 1600.
- 5. Johannes Opsopoeus; *Oracula Magica Zoroastris* 1599. This includes the Commentaries of Pletho and of Psellus in Latin.
- 6. Servatus Gallœus; *Sibulliakoi Chresmoi*, 1688.

Contains a version of the Oracles.

- Thomas Stanley. *The History of the Chaldaic Philosophy*, 1701. This treatise contains the Latin of Patricius, and the Commentaries of Pletho and Psellus in English.
- Johannes Alb. Fabricius, *Bibliotheca Græca*, 1705-7. *Quotes the Oracles.*
- Jacobus Marthanus, 1689. This version contains the Commentary of Gemistus Pletho.

- Thomas Taylor, *The Chaldæan Oracles*, in the *Monthly Magazine*, and published independently, 1806.
- *Bibliotheca Classica Latina;* A. Lemaire, volume 124, Paris, 1823.
- Isaac Preston Cory, *Ancient Fragments*, London, 1828. (A third edition of this work has been published, omitting the Oracles.)
- *Phœnix*, New York, 1835. A collection of curious old tracts, among which are the Oracles of Zoroaster, copied from Thomas Taylor and I. P. Cory; with an essay by Edward Gibbon.

---

1. Josephus, *contra Apion. I.*
2. Stephanus, *De Urbibus*.
3. *Vide* his Scholia on the *Cratylus* of Plato.

INTRODUCTION BY L. O.

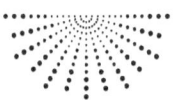

IT has been believed by many, and not without good reason, that these terse and enigmatic utterances enshrine a profound system of mystical philosophy, but that this system demands for its full discernment a refinement of faculty, involving, as it does, a discrete perception of immaterial essences.

It has been asserted that the Chaldæan Magi [1] preserved their occult learning among their race by continual tradition from Father to Son. Diodorus says: "They learn these things, not after the same fashion as the Greeks: for amongst the Chaldæans, philosophy is delivered by tradition in the family, the Son receiving it from his Father, being exempted from all other employment; and thus having their parents for their teachers, they learn all things fully and abundantly, believing more firmly what is communicated to them." [2]

The remains then of this oral tradition seems to exist in these Oracles, which should be studied in the light of the Kabalah and of Egyptian Theology. Students are aware that the Kabalah [3] is susceptible of extraordinary interpretation with the aid of the Tarot, resuming as the latter does, the very roots of Egyptian Theology. Had a similar course been adopted by commentators in the past, the Chaldæan system expounded in these Oracles would not have been distorted in the way it has been.

The foundation upon which the whole structure of the Hebrew Kabalah rests is an exposition of ten deific powers successively emanated by the Illimitable Light, which in their varying dispositions are considered as the key of all things. This divine procession in the form of Three Triads of Powers, synthesized in a tenth, is said to be extended through four worlds, denominated respectively Atziluth, Briah, Yetzirah and Assiah, a fourfold gradation from the subtil to the gross. This proposition in its metaphysical roots is pantheistic, though, if it may be so stated, mediately theistic; while the ultimate noumenon of all phenomena is the absolute Deity, whose ideation constitutes the objective Universe.

Now these observations apply strictly also to the Chaldæan system.

The accompanying diagrams sufficiently indicate the harmony and identity of the Chaldæan philosophy with the Hebrew Kabalah. It will be seen that the First Mind and the *Intelligible Triad*, Pater, Potentia, or Mater, and Mens, are allotted to the Intelligible

World of Supramundane Light: the "First Mind" represents the archetypal intelligence as an entity in the bosom of the Paternal Depth. This concentrates by reflection into the "Second Mind" representative of the Divine Power in the Empyræan World which is identified with the second great Triad of divine powers, known as *the Intelligible and at the same time Intellectual Triad:* the Æthereal World comprises the dual third Triad denominated *Intellectual:* while the fourth or Elementary World is governed by Hypezokos, or Flower of Fire, the actual builder of the world.

CHALDÆAN SCHEME.

The Intelligibles World of Supra-mundane Light	The Paternal Depth The First Mind
	——— The Intelligible Triad Pater: Mater or Potentia: Mens
	The Second Mind ———
Intelligibles and Intellectuals in the Empyræan World	Iynges Synoches Teletarchæ
Intellectuals in the Ethereal World	(The Third Mind.) Three Cosmagogi (Intellectual guides inflexible.) Three Amilicti (Implacable thunders).
Elementary World The Demiurgos of the Material Universe	Hypezokos (Flower of Fire) Effable, Essential and Elemental Orders

KABALISTIC SCHEME.

World of Atziluth or of God	The Boundless The Illimitable Light	Ain Suph. Ain Suph Aur A radiant triangle

	Kether (crown)	
World of Briah Divine Forces	Binah (Intelligence)	Chokmah (Wisdom)

	Geburah	Chesed
	Tiphereth	
World of Yetzirah or of Formation	Hod	Netzach.
	Yesod	

World of Assiah	Malkuth Ruled by
Material Form.	Adonai Melekh

The Earth-Matter

CHALDÆAN SCHEME OF BEINGS.

Representatives of the previous classes guiding our universe.

I. Hyperarchii--Archangels
II. Azonœi--Unzoned gods
III. Zonœi--Planetary Deities.

Higher demons: Angels

Human Souls

Lower demons, elementals

Fiery
Airy
Earthy
Watery

Evil demons
Lucifugous; the kliphoth

～

Chaldæan Theology contemplated three great divisions of supra-mundane things:—the First was *Eternal*, without beginning or end, being the "Paternal Depth," the bosom of the Deity. The Second was conceived to be that mode of being having beginning but no end; the Creative World or Empyræum falls under this head, abounding as it does in productions, but its source remaining superior to these. The third and last order of divine things had a beginning in time and will end, this is the transitory Ethereal World. Seven spheres extended through these three Worlds, *viz.*, one in the Empyræum or verging from it, three in the Ethereal and three in the Elementary Worlds, while the whole physical realm synthesized the foregoing. These seven spheres are not to be confounded with the Seven material Planets; although the latter are the physical representatives of the former, which can only be said to be material in the metaphysical sense of the term. Psellus professed to identify them but his suggestions are inadequate as Stanley pointed out. But Stanley, although disagreeing with Psellus, is nevertheless inconsistent upon this point, for although he explains the four - Worlds of the Chaldæans as successively noumenal to the physical realm, he obviously contradicts this in saying that one *corporeal* world is in the Empyræum.

Prior to the supramundane Light lay the "Paternal Depth," the Absolute Deity, containing all things "*in potentia*" and eternally immanent. This is analogous to the Ain Suph Aur of the Kabalah, three words of three letters, expressing three triads of Powers, which are subsequently translated into objectivity, and constitute the great Triadic Law sunder the direction of the Demiurgus, or artificer of the Universe.

In considering this schema, it must be remembered that the supramundane Light was regarded as the primal radiation from the Paternal Depth and the archetypal noumenon of the Empyræum, a universal, all-pervading—and, to human comprehension—ultimate essence. The Empyræum again, is a somewhat grosser though still highly subtilized Fire and creative source, in its turn the noumenon of the Formative or Ethereal World, as the latter is the noumenon of the Elementary World. Through these graduated media the conceptions of the Paternal Mind are ultimately fulfilled in time and space.

In some respects it is probable that the Oriental mind day is not much altered from what it was thousands of years ago, and much that now appears to us curious and phantastic in Eastern traditions, still finds responsive echo in the hearts and minds of a vast portion of mankind. A large number of thinkers and scientists in modern times have advocated tenets which, while not exactly similar, are parallel to ancient Chaldæan conceptions; this is exemplified in the notion that the operation of natural law in the Universe is controlled or operated by conscious and discriminating power which is co-ordinate with intelligence. It is but one step further to admit that forces are entities, to people the vast spaces of the Universe with the children of phantasy. Thus history repeats itself, and the old and the new alike reflect the multiform truth.

Without entering at length into the metaphysical aspect, it is important to notice the supremacy attributed to the "Paternal Mind." The intelligence of the Universe, poetically described as "energising before energy," establishes on high the primordial types or patterns of things which are to be, and, then inscrutably latent, vests the development of these in the

Rectores Mundorum, the divine Regents or powers already referred to. As it is said, "Mind is with Him, power with them."

The word "Intelligible" is used in the Platonic sense, to denote a mode of being, power or perception, transcending intellectual comprehension, *i.e.*, wholly distinct from, and superior to, ratiocination. The Chaldæans recognised three modes of perception, *viz.*, the testimony of the various senses, the ordinary processes of intellectual activity, and the intelligible conceptions before referred to. Each of these operations is distinct from the others, and, moreover, conducted in separate matrices, or vehicula. The anatomy of the Soul was, however, carried much farther than this, and, although in its ultimate radix recognised as identical with the divinity, yet in manifested being it was conceived to be highly complex. The Oracles speak of the "Paths of the Soul," the tracings of inflexible fire by which its essential parts are associated in integrity; while its various "summits," "fountains," and "vehicula," are all traceable by analogy with universal principles: This latter fact is, indeed, not the least remarkable feature of the Chaldæan system. Like several of the ancient cosmogonies, the principal characteristic of which seems to have been a certain adaptability to introversion, Chaldæan metaphysics synthesize most clearly in the human constitution.

In each of the Chaldæan Divine Worlds a trinity of divine powers operated, which synthetically constituted a fourth term. "In every World," says the Oracle, "a Triad shineth, of which the Monad is the ruling principle." These "Monads" are the divine Vice-gerents by which the Universe was conceived to be administered. Each of the four Worlds, *viz.*, the Empyræan, Ethereal, Elementary and Material, was presided over by a Supreme Power, itself in direct *rapport* with "the Father" and "moved by unspeakable counsels." These are clearly identical with the Kabalistic conception of the presidential heads of the four letters composing the Deity name in so many different languages. A parallel tenet is conveyed in the Oracle which runs: "There is a Venerable Name projected through the Worlds with a sleepless revolution." The Kabalah again supplies the key to this utterance, by regarding the Four Worlds as under the presidency of the four letters of the Venerable Name, a certain letter of the four being allotted to each World, as also was a special mode of writing the four-lettered name appropriate thereto; and, indeed in that system it is taught that the order of the Elements, both macrocosmic and microcosmic, on every plane, is directly controlled by the "revolution of the name." That Name is associated with the Æthers of the Elements and is thus considered as a Universal Law; it is the power which marshals the creative host, summed up in the Demiurgus, Hypezokos, or Flower of Fire.

Reference may here be made to the psychic anatomy of the human being according to Plato. He places the intellect in the head; the Soul endowed with some of the passions, such as fortitude, in the heart; while another Soul, of which the appetites, desires and grosser passions are its faculties, about the stomach and the spleen.

So, the Chaldæan doctrine as recorded by Psellus, considered man to be composed of three kinds of Souls, which may respectively be called:

- First, the Intelligible, or divine soul,
- Second, the Intellect or rational soul, and
- Third, the Irrational, or passional soul.

This latter was regarded as subject to mutation, to be dissolved and perish at the death of the body.

Of the Intelligible, or divine soul, the Oracles teach that "It is a bright fire, which, by the power of the Father, remaineth immortal, and is Mistress of Life;" its power may be dimly apprehended through regenerate phantasy and when the sphere of the Intellect has ceased to respond to the images of the passional nature.

Concerning the rational soul, the Chaldæans taught that it was possible for it to assimilate itself unto the divinity on the one hand, or the irrational soul on the other. "Things divine," we read, "cannot be obtained by mortals whose intellect is directed to the body alone, but those only who are stripped of their garments, arrive at the summit."

To the three Souls to which reference has been made, the Chaldæans moreover allotted three distinct vehicles: that of the divine Soul was immortal, that of the rational soul by approximation became so; while to the irrational soul was allotted what was called "the image," that is. the astral form of the physical body.

Physical life thus integrates three special modes of activity, which upon the dissolution of the body are respectively involved in the web of fate consequent upon incarnate energies in three-different destinies.

The Oracles urge men to devote themselves to things divine, and not to give way to the promptings of the irrational soul, for, to such as fail herein, it is significantly said, "Thy vessel the beasts of the earth shall inhabit."

The Chaldæans assigned the place of the Image, the vehicle of the irrational soul, to the Lunar Sphere; it is probable that by the Lunar Sphere was meant something more than the orb of the Moon, the whole sublunary region, of which the terrestrial earth is, as it were, the centre. At death, the rational Soul rose above the lunar influence, provided always the past permitted that happy release. Great importance was attributed to the way in which the physical life was passed during the sojourn of the Soul in the tenement of flesh, and frequent are the exhortations to rise to communion with those Divine powers, to which nought but the highest Theurgy can pretend.

"Let the immortal depth of your Soul lead you," says an Oracle, "but earnestly raise your eyes upwards." Taylor comments upon this in the following beautiful passage: "By the eyes are to be understood all the gnostic powers of the Soul, for when these are extended the Soul becomes replete with a more excellent life and divine illumination; and is, as it were, raised above itself."

Of the Chaldæan Magi it might be truly said that they "among dreams did first discriminate the truthful vision!" for they were certainly endowed with a far reaching perception both mental and spiritual; attentive to images, and fired with mystic fervours, they were something more than mere theorists, but were also practical exemplars of the philosophy they taught. Life on the plains of Chaldæa, with its mild nights and jewelled skies, tended to foster the interior unfoldment; in early life the disciples of the Magi learnt to resolve the Bonds of proscription and enter the immeasurable region. One Oracle assures us that, "The girders of the Soul, which give her breathing, are easy to be unloosed," and elsewhere we read of the "Melody of the Ether" and of the "Lunar clashings," experiences which testify to the reality of their occult methods.

The Oracles assert that the impressions of characters and other divine visions appear in the Ether. The Chaldæan philosophy recognized the ethers of the Elements as the subtil media through which the operation of the grosser elements is effected—by the grosser elements I mean what we know as Earth, Air, Water and Fire—the principles of dryness and moisture, of heat and cold. These subtil ethers are really the elements of the ancients, and seen at an early period to have been connected with the Chaldæan astrology, as the signs of the Zodiac were connected with them. The twelve signs of the Zodiac are permutations of the ethers of the elements—four elements with three variations each; and according to the preponderance of one or another elemental condition in the constitution of the individual, so were his natural inclinations deduced therefrom. Thus when in the astrological jargon it was said that a man had Aries rising, he was said to be of a fiery nature, his natural tendencies being active, energetic and fiery, for in the constitution of such a one the fiery ether predominates. And these ethers were stimulated, or endowed with a certain kind of vibration, by their Presidents, the Planets; these latter being thus suspended in orderly disposed zones. Unto the Planets, too, colour and sound were also attributed;, the planetary colours are connected with the ethers, and each of the Planetary forces was said to have special dominion over, or affinity with, one or other of the Zodiacal constellations. Communion with the hierarchies of these constellations formed part of the Chaldæan theurgy, and in a curious fragment it is said: "If thou often invokest it" (the celestial constellation called the Lion) "then when no longer is visible unto thee the Vault of the Heavens, when the Stars have lost their light the lamp of the Moon is veiled, the Earth abideth not, and around thee darts the lightning flame, then all things will appear to thee in the form of a Lion!" The Chaldæans, like the Egyptians, appear to have had a highly developed appreciation of colours, an evidence of their psychic susceptibility. The use of bright colours engenders the recognition of subsisting variety and stimulates that perception of the mind which energizes through imagination, or the operation of images. The Chaldæan method of Contemplation appears to have been to identify the self with the object of contemplation; this is of course identical with the process of Indian Yoga, and is an idea which appears replete with suggestion; as it is written, "He assimilates the images to himself, casting them around his own form." But we are told, "All divine natures are incorporeal, but bodies are bound in them for your sakes."

The subtil ethers, of which I have spoken, served in their turn as it were for the garment of the divine Light; for the Oracles teach that beyond these again " A solar world and endless Light subsist! " This Divine Light was the object of all veneration. Do not think that what was intended thereby was the Solar Light we know: "The inerratic sphere of the Starless above" is an unmistakable expression and therein "the more true Sun " has place: Theosophists will appreciate the significance of "the more true Sun," for according to *The Secret Doctrine* the Sun we see is but the physical vehicle of a more transcendent splendour.

Some strong Souls were able to reach up to the Light by their own power: "The mortal who approaches the fire shall have Light from the divinity, and unto the persevering mortal the blessed immortals are swift." But what of those of a lesser stature? Were they, by inability, precluded from such illumination? "Others," we read, "even when asleep, He makes fruitful from his own Strength." That is to say, some men acquire divine knowledge through communion with Divinity in sleep. This idea has given rise to some of the most magnificent contributions to later literature; it has since been thoroughly elaborated by

Porphyry and Synesius. The eleventh Book of the *Metamorphoses* of Apuleius and the *Vision of Scipio* ably vindicate this; and, although no doubt every Christian has heard that "He giveth unto his beloved in sleep," few, indeed, realise the possibility underlying that conception.

What, it may be asked, were the views of the Chaldæans with respect to terrestrial life: Was it a spirit of pessimism, which led them to hold this in light esteem? Or, should we not rather say that the keynote of their philosophy was an immense spiritual optimism? It appears to me that the latter is the more true interpretation. They realised that beyond the confines of matter lay a more perfect existence, a truer realm of which terrestrial administration is but a too often travestied reflection. They sought, as we seek now, the Good, the Beautiful and the True, but they did not hasten to the Outer in the thirst for sensation, but with a finer perception realised the true Utopia to be within.

And the first step in that admirable progress was a return to the simple life; hardly, indeed, a return, for most of the Magi were thus brought up from birth. [4] The hardihood engendered by the rugged life, coupled with that wisdom which directed their association, rendered these children of Nature peculiarly receptive of Nature's Truths. "Stoop not down," says the Oracle, "to the darkly splendid World, For a precipice lieth beneath the Earth, a descent of seven steps, and therein is established the throne of an evil and fatal force. Stoop not down unto that darkly splendid world, Defile not thy brilliant flame with the earthly dross of matter, Stoop not down for its splendour is but seeming, It is but the habitation of the Sons of the Unhappy." No more beautiful formulation of the Great Truth that the exterior and sensuous life is death to the highest energies of the Soul could possibly have been uttered: but to such as by purification and the practice of virtue rendered themselves. worthy, encouragement was given, for, we read, "The Higher powers build up the body of the holy man."

The law of Karma was as much a feature of the Chaldæan philosophy as it is of the Theosophy of today: from a passage in *Ficinus*, we read, "The Soul perpetually runs and passes through all things in a certain space of time, which being performed it is presently compelled to pass back again through all things and unfold a similar web of generation in the World, according to Zoroaster, who thinks that as often as the same causes return, the same effects will in like manner return."

This is of course the explanation of the proverb that "History repeats itself," and is very far from the superstitious view of fate. Here each one receives his deserts according to merit or demerit, and these are the bonds of life; but the Oracles say, "Enlarge not thy destiny," and they urge men to "Explore the River of the Soul, so that although you have become a servant to body, you may again rise to the Order from which you descended, joining works to sacred reason!"

To this end we are commended to learn the Intelligible which exists beyond the mind, that divine portion of the being which exists beyond Intellect: and this it is only possible to grasp with the flower of the mind. "Understand the intelligible with the extended flame of an extended intellect." To Zoroaster also was attributed the utterance "who knows himself knows all things in himself;" while it is elsewhere suggested that "The paternal Mind has sowed symbols in the Soul." But such priceless knowledge was possible only to the Theurgists Who, we are told, "fall not so as to be ranked with the herd that are in subjection to fate." The divine light cannot radiate in an imperfect microcosm, even as the Clouds obscure the Sun; for of such as make ascent to the most divine of speculations in a confused and disordered manner, with unhallowed lips, or unwashed feet, the progressions are imperfect, the impulses are vain and the paths are dark.

Although destiny, our destiny, may be " written in the Stars" yet it was the mission of the divine Soul to raise the human Soul above the circle of necessity, and the Oracles give Victory to that Masterly Will, which

> *"Hews the wall with might of magic,*
> *Breaks the palisade in pieces,*
> *Hews to atoms seven pickets . . .*
> *Speaks the Master words of knowledge! "*

The means taken to that consummation consisted in the training of the Will and the elevation, of the imagination, a divine power which controls consciousness: Believe yourself to be above body, and you are," says the Oracle; it might have added "Then shall regenerate phantasy disclose the symbols of the Soul."

But it is said "On beholding yourself fear!" *i.e.*, . the imperfect self.

Everything must be viewed as ideal by him who would understand the ultimate perfection.

Will is the grand agent in the mystic progress; its rule is all potent over the nervous system. By Will the fleeting vision is fixed on the treacherous waves of the astral Light; by Will the consciousness is impelled to commune with the divinity: yet there is not One Will, but three Wills—the Wills, namely, of the Divine, the Rational and Irrational Souls—to harmonize these is the difficulty.

It is selfishness which impedes the radiation of Thought, and attaches to body. This is scientifically true and irrespective of sentiment, the selfishness which reaches beyond the necessities of body is pure vulgarity.

A picture which to the cultured eye beautifully portrays a given subject, nevertheless appears to the savage a confused patchwork of streaks, so the extended perceptions of a citizen of the Universe are not grasped by those whose thoughts dwell within the sphere of the personal life.

The road to the *Summum Bonum* lies therefore through self-sacrifice, the sacrifice of the lower to the higher, for behind that Higher Self lies the concealed form of the Antient of Days, the synthetical Being of Divine Humanity.

These things are grasped by Soul; the song of the Soul is alone heard in the adytum of God-nourished Silence!

---

1. This powerful Guild was the guardian of Chaldæan philosophy, which exceeded the bounds of their country, and diffused itself into Persia and Arabia that borders upon it; for which reason the learning of the Chaldæans, Persians and Arabians is comprehended under the general title of Chaldæan.
2. *Diodorus, lib. I.*
3. *Vide Kabalah Denudata*, by MacGregor Mathers.
4. They renounced rich attire and the wearing of gold. Their raiment was white upon occasion; their beds the ground, and their food nothing but herbs, cheese and bread.

THE ORACLES OF ZOROASTER

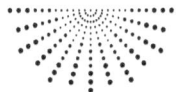

CAUSE. GOD.

| FATHER. | MIND. | FIRE. |
| MONAD. | DYAD. | TRIAD. |

1. But God is He having the head of the Hawk. The same is the first, incorruptible, eternal, unbegotten, indivisible, dissimilar: the dispenser of all good; indestructible; the best of the good, the Wisest of the wise; He is the Father of Equity and Justice, self-taught, physical, perfect, and wise—He who inspires the Sacred Philosophy.

Eusebius. *Præparatio Evangelica*, liber. I., chap. X.

This Oracle does not appear in either of the ancient collections, nor in the group of oracles given by any of the mediæval oc-

cultists. Cory seems to have been the first to discover it in the voluminous writings of Eusebius, who attributes the authorship to the Persian Zoroaster

~

2. Theurgists assert that He is a God and celebrate him as both older and younger, as a circulating and eternal God, as understanding the whole number of all things moving in the World, and moreover infinite through his power and energizing a spiral force.

Proclus on the *Timæus* of Plato, 244. Z. or T.

The Egyptian Pantheon had an Elder and a Younger Horus— a God—son of Osiris and Isis. Taylor suggests that He refers to Kronos, Time, or Chronos, as the later Platonists wrote the name. Kronos, or Saturnus, of the Romans, was son of Uranos and Gaia, husband of Rhea, father of Zeus.

~

3. The God of the Universe, eternal, limitless, both young and old, having a spiral force.

Cory includes this Oracle in his collection, but he gives no authority for it.

Lobeck doubted its authenticity.

~

4. For the Eternal Æon [1]—according to the Oracle—is the cause of never failing life, of unwearied power and unsluggish energy.

Taylor.—T.

5. Hence the inscrutable God is called silent by the divine ones, and is said to consent with Mind, and to be known to human souls through the power of the Mind alone.

Proclus in *Theologiam Platonis*, 321. T.

Inscrutable. Taylor gives "stable;" perhaps "incomprehensible" is better.

6. The Chaldæans call the God Dionysos (or Bacchus), Iao in the Phœnician tongue (instead of the Intelligible Light), and he is also called Sabaoth, [2] signifying that he is above the Seven poles, that is the Demiurgos.

Lydus, *De Mensibus*, 83. T.

7. Containing all things in the one summit of his own Hyparxis, He Himself subsists wholly beyond.

> Proclus in *Theologiam Platonis*, 212. T.

Hyparxis, is generally deemed to mean "Subsistence." Hupar is Reality *as distinct from* appearance; *Huparche is a Beginning.*

∽

8. Measuring and bounding all things.

> Proclus in *Theologiam Platonis*, 386. T.

"Thus he speaks the words," is omitted by Taylor and Cory, but present in the Greek.

∽

9. For nothing imperfect emanates from the Paternal Principle,

> *Psellus*, 38; *Pletho. Z.*

This implies—but only from a succedent emanation.

∽

10. The Father effused not Fear, but He infused persuasion.

> *Pletho. Z.*

11. The Father hath apprehended Himself, and hath not restricted his Fire to his own intellectual power.

Psellus, 30; *Pletho*, 33. Z.

Taylor gives:—The Father hath hastily withdrawn Himself, but hath not shut up his own Fire in his intellectual power.

The Greek text has no word "hastily," and as to withdrawn—Arpazo means, grasp or snatch, but also "apprehend with the mind."

12. Such is the Mind which is energized before energy, while yet it had not gone forth, but abode in the Paternal Depth, and in the Adytum of God nourished silence.

Proc. in *Tim.*, 167. T.

13. All things have issued from that one Fire.

The Father perfected all things, and delivered them over to the Second Mind, whom all Nations of Men call the First.

Psellus, 24; *Pletho*, 30. Z.

14. The Second Mind conducts the Empyrean World.

Damascius, *De Principiis*. T.

15. What the Intelligible saith, it saith by understanding.

Psellus, 35. Z.

16. Power is with them, but Mind is from Him.

Proclus in *Platonis Theologiam*, 365. T.

17. The Mind of the Father riding on the subtle Guiders, which glitter with the tracings of inflexible and relentless Fire.

Proclus on the *Cratylus of Plato*. T.

18. . . . . . After the Paternal Conception
I the Soul reside, a heat animating all things.
. . . . For he placed

The Intelligible in the Soul, and the Soul in dull body,

Even so the Father of Gods and Men placed them in us.

Proclus in *Tim. Plat.*, 124.. Z. or T.

19. Natural works co-exist with the intellectual light of the Father. For it is the Soul which adorned the vast Heaven, and which adorneth it after the Father, but her dominion is established on high.

Proclus in Tim., 106. Z. or T.

Dominion, krata: some copies give kerata, horns.

20. The Soul, being a brilliant Fire, by the power of the Father remaineth immortal, and is Mistress of Life, and filleth up the many recesses of the bosom of the World.

Psellus, 28; *Pletho*, 11. Z.

21. The channels being intermixed, therein she performeth the works of incorruptible Fire.

Proclus in *Politico*, p. 399. Z. or T.

22. For not in Matter did the Fire which is in the first beyond enclose His active Power, but in Mind; for the framer of the Fiery World is the Mind of Mind.

Proclus in Theologian, 333, and Tim., 157. T.

23. Who first sprang from Mind, clothing the one Fire with the other Fire, binding them together, that he might mingle the fountainous craters, while preserving unsullied the brilliance of His own Fire.

Proclus in Parm. Platonis. T.

24. And thence a Fiery Whirlwind drawing down the brilliance of the flashing flame, penetrating the abysses of the Universe; for from thence downwards do extend their wondrous rays.

Proclus in Theologian Platonis, 171 and 172. T.

25. The Monad first existed, and the Paternal Monad still subsists.

Proclus in Euclidem, 27. T.

26. When the Monad is extended, the Dyad is generated.

Proclus in Euclidemi, 27. T.

Note that" What the Pythagoreans signify by Monad, Duad and Triad, or Plato by Bound, Infinite and Mixed; that the Oracles of the Gods intend by Hyparxis, Power and Energy."

Damascius *De Principiis*. Taylor.

~

27. And beside Him is seated the Dyad which glitters with intellectual sections, to govern all things and to order everything not ordered.

Proclus in *Platonis Theologiam*, 376. T.

28. The Mind of the Father said that all things should be cut into Three, whose Will assented, and immediately all things were so divided.

Proclus in *Parmen*. T.

29. The Mind of the Eternal Father said into Three, governing all things by Mind.

Proclus, *Timæus of Plato*. T.

30. The Father mingled every Spirit from this Triad.

Lydus, *De Mensibus*, 20. Taylor.

31. All things are supplied from the bosom of this Triad.

Lydus, *De Mensibus*, 20. Taylor.

32. All things are governed and subsist in this Triad.

Proclus in I. Alcibiades. T.

33. For thou must know that all things bow before the Three Supernals.

Damascius, *De Principiis.* T.

34. From thence floweth forth the Form of the Triad, being preëxistent; not the first Essence, but that whereby all things are measured.

Anon. Z. or T.

35. And there appeared in it Virtue and Wisdom, and multiscient Truth.

Anon. Z. or T.

36. For in each World shineth the Triad, over which the Monad ruleth.

Damascius in *Parmenidem.* T.

37. The First Course is Sacred, in the middle place courses the Sun, [3] in the third the Earth is heated by the internal fire.

Anon. Z. or T.

38. Exalted upon High and animating Light, Fire Ether and Worlds.

Simplicius in his *Physica*, 143. Z. or T.

---

1. *"For the First Æon, the Eternal one," or as Taylor gives, "Eternity."*
2. *This word is Chaldee, TzBAUT, meaning hosts; but there is also a word SHBOH, meaning The Seven.*
3. *Jones gives Sun from Helios, but some Greek versions give Herios, which Cory translates, air.*

IDEAS

INTELLIGIBLES, INTELLECTUALS, IYNGES, SYNOCHES, TELETARCHÆ, FOUNTAINS, PRINCIPLES, HECATE AND DÆMONS

39. The Mind of the Father whirled forth in re-echoing roar, comprehending by invincible Will Ideas omniform; which flying forth from that one fountain issued; for from the Father alike, was the Will and the End (by which are they connected with the Father according to alternating life, through varying vehicles). But they were divided asunder, being by Intellectual Fire distributed into other Intellectuals. For the King of all previously placed before the polymorphous World a Type, intellectual, incorruptible, the imprint of whose form is sent forth through the World, by which the Universe shone forth decked with Ideas all various, of which the foundation is One, One and alone. From this the others rush forth distributed and separated through the various bodies of the Universe, and are borne in swarms through its vast abysses, ever whirling forth in illimitable radiation.

They are intellectual conceptions from the Paternal Fountain partaking abundantly of the brilliance of Fire in the culmination of unresting Time.

But the primary self-perfect Fountain of the Father poured forth these primogenial Ideas.

Proclus in Parmenidem. *Z. or T.*

40. These being many, descend flashingly upon the shining Worlds, and in them are contained the Three Supernals.

Damascius in Parmenidem. *T*

41. They are the guardians of the works of the Father, and of the One Mind, the Intelligible.

Proclus in Theologiam Platonis, *205. T.*

42. All things subsist together in the Intelligible World.

Damascius, De Principiis. *T.*

43. But all Intellect understandeth the Deity, for Intellect existeth not without the Intelligible, neither apart from Intellect doth the Intelligible subsist.

Damascius. Z. or T.

44. For Intellect existeth not without the Intelligible; apart from it, it subsisteth not.

Proclus, *Th. Pl.*, 172. Z. or T.

45. By Intellect He containeth the Intelligibles and introduceth the Soul into the Worlds.

46. By Intellect he containeth the Intelligibles, and introduceth Sense into the Worlds.

Proclus in *Crat.* T.

47. For this Paternal Intellect, which comprehendeth the Intelligibles and adorneth things ineffable, hath sowed symbols through the World.

Proclus in *Cratylum.* T.

48. This Order is the beginning of all section.

Dam., *De Prin.* T.

49. The Intelligible is the principle of all section.

Damascius, *De Principiis.* T.

50. The Intelligible is as food to that which understandeth.

Dam., *De Prin.* T.

51. The oracles concerning the Orders exhibits It as prior to the Heavens, as ineffable, and they add—It hath Mystic Silence.

Proclus in *Cratylum*. T.

52. The oracle calls the Intelligible causes Swift, Mid asserts that, proceeding from the Father, they rush again unto Him.

Proclus in *Cratylum*. T.

53. Those Natures are both Intellectual and Intelligible, which, themselves possessing Intellection, are the objects of Intelligence to others.

Proclus, *Theologiam Platonis*. T.

The Second Order of the Platonist philosophy was the "Intelligible and Intellectual Triad." Among the Chaldæans this order includes the Iynges, Synoches and Teletarchs. The Intellectual Triad of the later Platonists corresponds to the Fountains, Fontal Fathers or Cosmagogi of the Chaldæans.

∼

54. The Intelligible Iynges themselves understand from the Father; by Ineffable counsels being moved so as to understand.

Psellus, 41; *Pletho*, 31. Z.

55. Because it is the Operator, because it is the Giver of Life Bearing Fire, because it filleth the Life-producing bosom of Hecaté; and it instilleth into the Synoches the enlivening strength of Fire, endued with mighty Power.

Proclus in Tim., 128. T.

56. He gave His own Whirlwinds to guard the Supernals, mingling the proper force of His own strength in the Synoches.

Dam., De Prin. T.

57. But likewise as many as serve the material Synoches.

T.

58. The Teletarchs are comprehended in the Synoches.

Dam., De Prin. T.

59. Rhea, the Fountain and River of the Blessed Intellectuals, having first received the powers of all things in Her Ineffable Bosom, pours forth perpetual Generation upon all things.

Proc. in Crat. T

60. For it is the bound of the Paternal Depth, and the Fountain of the Intellectuals.

Dam., *De Prin.* T.

61. For He is a Power of circumlucid strength, glittering with Intellectual Sections.

Dam. T.

62 . He glittereth with Intellectual Sections, and hath filled all things with love.

Dam. T.

63. Unto the Intellectual Whirlings of Intellectual Fire, all things are subservient, through the persuasive counsel of the Father.

Proc. in *Parm.* T.

64. O! how the World hath inflexible Intellectual Rulers.

65. The source of the Hecaté correspondeth with that of the Fontal Fathers.

T.

66. From Him leap forth the Amilicti the all-relentless thunders, and the whirlwind receiving Bosoms of the all-splendid Strength of Hecaté Father-begotten; and

He who encircleth the Brilliance of Fire; And the Strong Spirit of the Poles, all fiery beyond.

Proc. in *Crat*. T.

67. There is another Fountain, which leadeth the Empyræan World.

Proc. in *Tim*. Z. or T.

68. The Fountain of Fountains, and the boundary of all fountains.

Dam., *De Prin*.

69. Under two Minds the Life-generating fountain of Souls is comprehended.

Dam., *De Prin*. T.

70. Beneath them exists the Principal One of the Immaterials.

Darn. in *Parm*. Z. or T.

Following the Intellectual Triad was the Demiurgos, from whom proceeded the Effable and Essential Orders including all sorts of Dæmons, and the Elementary World.

71. Father begotten Light, which alone hath gathered from the strength of the Father the Flower of mind, and hath the power of understanding the Paternal mind, and Both instil into all Fountains and Principles the power of understanding and the function of ceaseless revolution.

Proc. in *Tim.*, 242.

72. All fountains and principles whirl round and always remain' in a ceaseless revolution.

Proc. in *Parm.* Z. or T.

73. The Principles, which have understood the Intelligible works of the Father, He hath clothed in sensible works and bodies, being intermediate links existing to connect the Father with Matter, rendering apparent the Images of unapparent Natures, and inscribing the Unapparent in the Apparent frame of the World.

Dam., *De Prin.* Z. or T.

74. Typhon, Echidna, and Python, being the progeny of Tartaros and Gaia, who were united by Uranos, form, as it were, a certain Chaldæan Triad, the Inspector and Guardian of all the disordered fabrications.

Olymp. in *Phæd.* T.

75. There are certain Irrational Demons (mindless elementals), which derive their subsistence from the Aërial Rulers; wherefore the Oracle saith, Being the Charioteer of the Aërial, Terrestrial and Aquatic Dogs.

Olymp. in Phæd. T.

76. The Aquatic when applied to Divine Natures signifies a Government inseparable from Water, and hence the Oracle calls the Aquatic Gods, Water Walkers:

Proc. in Tim., 270. T.

77. There are certain Water Elementals whom Orpheus calls Nereides, dwelling in the more elevated exhalations of Water, such as appear in damp, cloudy Air, whose bodies are sometimes seen (as Zoroaster taught) by more acute eyes, especially in Persia and Africa.

Ficinus de Immortalitate Animæ, 123. T.

PARTICULAR SOULS

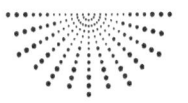

SOUL, LIFE, MAN

78. The Father conceived ideas, and all mortal bodies were animated by Him.

Proc. in Tim., 336. T.

79. For the Father of Gods and men placed the Mind (nous) in the Soul (psyche); and placed both in the (human) body.

80. The Paternal Mind hath sowed symbols in the Soul.

Psell., 26; *Pletho*, 6.. Z.

81. Having mingled the Vital Spark from two according substances, Mind and Divine Spirit, as a third to these He added Holy Love, the venerable Charioteer uniting all things.

Lyd. De Men., 3.

82. Filling the Soul with profound Love.

Proc. in *Pl. Theol*, 4. Z or T.

83. The Soul of man does in a manner clasp God to herself. Having nothing mortal, she is wholly inebriated with God. For she glorieth in the harmony under which the mortal body subsisteth.

Psellus, 17; *Pletho*, 10. Z.

84. The more powerful Souls perceive Truth through themselves, and are of -a more inventive Nature. Such Souls are saved through their own strength, according to the Oracle.

Proclus in I. *Alc.* Z.

85. The Oracle saith that Ascending Souls sing a Pæan.

Olymp. in *Phæd.* Z or T.

86. Of all Souls, those certainly are superlatively blessed, which are poured forth from Heaven to Earth; and they are happy, and have ineffable stamina, as many as proceed from Thy Splendid Self, O King, or from Jove Himself, under the strong necessity of Mithus.

Synes. De Insom, 153. Z or T.

Query Mithras.

∽

87. The Souls of those who quit the body violently are most pure.

Psellus, 27. Z.

88. The girders of the Soul, which give her breathing, are easy to be unloosed.

Psellus, 32; Pletho, 8. Z.

89. For when you see a Soul set free, the Father sendeth another, that the number may be complete.

Z. or T.

90. Understanding the works of the Father, they avoid the shameless Wing of Fate; they are placed in God, drawing forth strong light-bearers, descending from the Father, from whom as they descend, the

Soul gathereth of the empyræan fruits the soul-nourishing flower.

Proc. in *Tim.*, 321. Z. or T.

91. This Animastic Spirit which blessed men have called the Pneumatic Soul, becometh a god, an all-various Dæmon, and an Image (disembodied), and in this form of Soul suffereth her punishments The Oracles, too, accord with this account; for they assimilate the employment of the Soul in Hades, to the delusive visions of a dream.

Synesius *De Insom.* Z. or T.

The word Dæmon in the original meaning of the term did not necessarily mean a bad Spirit, and was as often applied to pure spirits as to impure.

Compare the Eastern doctrine of Devachan, a stage of pleasing illusion after death.

∼

92. One life after another, from widely distributed sources. Passing from above, through to the opposite part; through the Centre of the Earth; and to the fifth middle, fiery centre, where the life-bearing fire descendeth as far as the material world.

Z. or T.

93. Water is a symbol of life; hence Plato and the gods before Plato, call it (the Soul) at one time the whole water of vivification, and at another time a certain fountain of it.

Proc. in *Tim.*, 318. Z.

94. O Man, of a daring nature, thou subtle production.

Psell., 12; *Pletho*, 21. Z,

95. For thy vessel the beasts of the Earth shall inhabit.

Psell., 36; *Pletho*, 7. Z.

Vessel is the body in which the Nous—thou, dwellest for a time.

96. Since the Soul perpetually runs and passes through many experiences in a certain space of time; which being performed, it is presently compelled to. pass back again through all things, and unfold a similar web of generation in the World, according to Zoroaster, who thinketh that as often as the same causes return, the same effects will in like manner be sure to ensue.

Ficin. *De Im. An.*, 129. Z.

97. According to Zoroaster, in us the ethereal vestment of the Soul perpetually revolves (reincarnates).

Ficin. *De Im. An.*, 131. Z.

98. The Oracles delivered by the Gods celebrate the essential fountain of every Soul; the Empyrean, the Ethereal and the Material. This fountain they separate from (Zoogonothea) the vivifying Goddess (Rhea), from whom (suspending the whole of Fate) they make two series or orders; the one animastic, or belonging to the Soul, and the other belonging to Fate. They assert that the Soul is derived front the animastic series, but that sometimes it becometh subservient to Fate, when passing into an irrational condition of being,. it becometh subject to Fate instead of to Providence.

Proclus *de Providentia* apud Fabricium in *Biblioth. Græca.*, vol. 8, 486. Z. or T.

MATTER

THE WORLD—AND NATURE

99. The Matrix containing all things.

T.

100. Wholly divisible, and yet indivisible.

101. Thence abundantly springeth forth the generations of multifarious Matter.

Proc. in *Tim.*, 118. T.

102. These frame atoms, sensible forms, corporeal bodies, and things destined to matter.

Dam, *De Prin*. T.

103. The Nymphs of the Fountains, and all the Water Spirits, and terrestrial, aërial and astral forms, are the Lunar Riders and Rulers of all Matter, the Celestial, the Starry, and that which lieth in the Abysses.

Lydus.

104. According to the Oracles, Evil is more feeble than Non-entity.

Proc. *de Prov.* Z. or T.

105. We learn that Matter pervadeth the whole world, as the Gods also assert.

Proc., *Tim.*, 142. Z. or T.

106. All Divine Natures are incorporeal, but bodies are bound to them for your sakes. Bodies not being able to contain incorporeals, by reason of the Corporeal Nature, in which ye are concentrated.

Proc. in *Pl. Polit.*, 359. Z. or T.

107. For the Paternal Self-begotten Mind, understanding His works sowed in all, the fiery bonds of love, that all things might continue loving for an infinite time. That the connected series of things might intellectually remain in the Light of the Father; that the elements of the World might continue their course in mutual attraction.

Proc. in *Tim.*, 155. T.

108. The Maker of all things, self-operating, framed the World. And there was a certain Mass of Fire: all these things Self-Operating He produced, that the Body of the Universe might be conformed, that the World might be manifest, and not appear membranous,

Proc. in *Tim.*, 154. Z. or T.

109. For He assimilateth the images to himself, casting them around his own form.

110. For they are an imitation of his Mind, but that which is fabricated hath something of Body.

Proc. in *Tim.*, 87. Z or. T.

111. There is a Venerable Name, with a sleepless revolution, leaping forth into the worlds, through the rapid tones of the Father.

Proc. in *Crat.* Z. or T.

112. The Ethers of the Elements therefore are there.

Olympiodorus in *Phæd.* Z. or T.

113. The Oracles assert that the types of Characters, and of other Divine visions appear in the Ether (or Astral Light).

Simp. in *Phys.*, 144. Z. or T.

114. In this the things without figure are figured.

Simp. in *Phys.*, 143. Z. or T.

115. The Ineffable and Effable impressions of the World.

116. The Light hating World, and the winding currents by which many are drawn down.

Proc. in *Tim.*, 339. Z. or T

117. He maketh the whole World of Fire, Air,. Water, and Earth, and of the all-nourishing Ether.

Z. or T.

118. Placing Earth in the middle, but Water below the Earth, and Air above both these.

Z. or T.

119. He fixed a vast multitude of un-wandering Stars, not by a strain laborious and hurtful, but with stability void of movement, forcing Fire forward into Fire.

Proc. in *Tim.*, 280. Z. or T.

120. The Father congregated the Seven Firmaments of the Kosmos, circumscribing the Heavens with convex form.

Dam. in *Parm.* Z, or T.

121. He constituted a Septenary of wandering Existences (the Planetary globes).

Z. or T.

122. Suspending their disorder in Well-disposed Zones.

Z. or T.

123. He made them six in number, and for the Seventh He cast into the midst thereof the Fiery Sun.

Proc. in *Tim.*, 280. Z. or T.

124. The Centre from which all (lines) which way soever are equal.

Proc. in *Euclidem*.

125. And that the Swift Sun doth pass as ever around a Centre.

Proc. in *Plat. Th.*, 317. Z. or T.

126. Eagerly urging itself towards that Centre of resounding Light.

Proc. in *Tim.*, 236. T.

127. The Vast Sun, and the Brilliant Moon.

128. As rays of Light his locks flow forth, ending in acute points.

Proc. in *Pl. Pol.* 387. T.

129. And of the Solar Circles, and of the Lunar, clashings, and of. the Aërial Recesses; the Melody of Ether, and of the Sun, and of the phases of the Moon, and of the Air.

Proc. in *Tim.*, 257. Z. or T.

130. The most mystic of discourses informs us that His wholeness is in the Supra-mundane Orders for there a Solar World and Boundless Light subsist, as, the Oracles of the Chaldæans affirm.

Proc. in *Tim.*, 264. Z. or T.

131. The Sun more true measureth all things by time, being itself the time of time, according to the Oracle of the Gods concerning it.

Proc. in Tim., 249. Z. or T.

132. The Disk (of the Sun) is borne in the Starless.. realm above the Inerratic Sphere; and hence he is, not in the midst of the Planets, but of the Three Worlds, according to the telestic Hypothesis.

Jul., *Crat.*, 5, 334. Z. or T.

133. The Sun is a Fire, the Channel of Fire, and the dispenser of Fire.

Proc. in Tim., 141. Z. or T.

134. Hence Kronos, The Sun as Assessor beholds the true pole.

135. The Ethereal Course, and the vast motion of the Moon, and the Aërial fluxes.

Proclus in *Tim.*, 257. Z. or T.

136. O Ether, Sun, and Spirit of the Moon, ye are the chiefs of the Air.

Proc. in Tim., 257. Z. or T.

137. And the wide Air, and the Lunar Course, and the Pole of the Sun.

Proc. in *Tim.*, 257. Z. or T.

138. For the Goddess bringeth forth the Vast Sun, and the lucent Moon.

139. She collecteth it, receiving the Melody of Ether, and of the Sun, and of the Moon, and of whatsoever things are contained in the Air.

140. Unwearied Nature ruleth over the Worlds and works, that the Heavens drawing downward might run an eternal course, and that the other periods of the Sun, Moon, Seasons, Night and Day, might be accomplished.

Proc. in *Tim.*, 4, 323. Z. or T.

141. And above the shoulders of that Great Goddess, is Nature in her vastness exalted.

Proc. in *Tim.*, 4. T.

142. The most celebrated of the Babylonians, together with Ostanes and Zoroaster, very properly call the starry Spheres "Herds"; whether because these alone among corporeal magnitudes, are perfectly carried about around a Centre, or in conformity to the Oracles, because they are considered by them as in a certain respect the bands and collectors of physical reasons, which they likewise call in their sacred discourse "Herds" (agelous) and by the insertion of a

gamma (aggelous) Angels. Wherefore the Stars which preside over each of these herds are considered to be Deities or Dæmons, similar to the Angels, and are called Archangels; and they are seven in number.

Anon. in *Theologumenis Arithmeticis*. Z.

Daimon in Greek meant "a Spirit," not "a bad Spirit."

∽

143. Zoroaster calls the congruities of material forms to the ideals of the Soul of the World—Divine Allurements.

Ficinus, *de Vit. Cæl. Comp.* Z.

MAGICAL AND PHILOSOPHICAL PRECEPTS

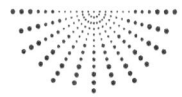

144. Direct not thy mind to the vast surfaces of the Earth; for the Plant of Truth grows not upon the ground. Nor measure the motions of the Sun, collecting rules, for be is carried by the Eternal Will of the Father, and not for your sake alone. Dismiss (from your mind) the impetuous course of the Moon, for she moveth always by the power of necessity. The progression of the Stars was not generated for your sake. The wide aërial flight of birds gives no true knowledge nor the dissection of the entrails of victims; they are all mere toys, the basis of mercenary fraud:, flee from these if you would enter the sacred paradise of piety, where Virtue, Wisdom and Equity are assembled.

Psel., 4. Z.

145. Stoop not down unto the Darkly-Splendid World; wherein continually lieth a faithless Depth, and Hades wrapped in clouds, delighting in unintellible images, precipitous, winding, a black ever-rolling Abyss; ever espousing a Body unluminous, formless and void.

Synes., *de Insom.*, 140. Z. or T.

146. Stoop not down, for a precipice lieth beneath the Earth, reached by a descending Ladder which hath Seven Steps, and therein is established the Throne of an evil and fatal force.

Psell., 6; *Pletho*, 2. Z.

147. Stay not on the Precipice with the dross of Matter, for there is a place for thy Image in a realm ever splendid.

Psell., 1, 2; *Pletho*, 14; *Synesius*, 140. Z.

148. Invoke not the visible Image of the Soul of Nature.

Psell., 15; *Pletho*, 23. Z.

149. Look not upon Nature, for her name is fatal.

Proc. in *Plat. Th.*, 143. Z.

150. It becometh you not to behold them before your body is initiated, since by alway alluring they seduce the souls from the sacred mysteries.

Proc. in I. *Alcib.* Z. or T.

151. Bring her not forth, lest in departing she retain something.

Psell., 3; *Pletho*, 15. Z.

Taylor says that "her" refers to the human soul.

152. Defile not the Spirit, nor deepen a superficies.

Psell., 19; *Pletho*, 13. Z.

153. Enlarge not thy Destiny.

Psell., 37; *Pletho*, 4.

154. Not hurling, according to the Oracle, a transcendent foot towards piety.

Dam. in *Vitam Isidore. ap. Suidam* Z. or T.

155. Change not the barbarous Names of Evocation for-there are sacred Names in every language which are given by God, having in the Sacred Rites a Power Ineffable.

Psell., 7. *Nicephotus*. Z. or T.

156. Go not forth when the Lictor passeth by.

Picus de Mirandula, *Concl.* Z.

157. Let fiery hope nourish you upon the Angelic plane.

Olymp. in *Phæd*. Proc. in *Alcib*. Z. or T.

158. The conception of the glowing Fire hath the first rank, for the mortal who approacheth that Fire shall have Light from God; and unto the persevering mortal the Blessed Immortals are swift.

Proc. in *Tim.*, 65. Z. or T.

159. The Gods exhort us to understand the radiating form of Light.

Proc. in *Crat.* Z. or T.

160. It becometh you to hasten unto the Light, and to the Rays of the Father, from whom was sent unto you a Soul (Psyche) endued with much mind (Nous).

Psell., 33. *Pletho*, 6. Z.

161. Seek Paradise.

Psell., 41. *Pletho*, 27. Z.

162. Learn the Intelligible for it subsisteth beyond the Mind.

Psell., 41. *Pletho*, 27. Z.

163. There is a certain Intelligible One, whom it becometh-you to understand with the Flower of Mind.

Psell., 31. *Pletho*, 28. Z.

164. But the Paternal Mind accepteth not the aspiration of the soul until she hath passed out of her oblivious state, and pronounceth the Word, regaining the Memory of the pure paternal Symbol.

Psell., 39. *Pletho*, 5. Z.

165. Unto some He gives the ability to receive the Knowledge of Light; and others, even when asleep, he makes fruitful from His own strength.

Synes., *de Insomn*, 135. Z. or T.

166. It is not proper to understand that Intelligible One with vehemence, but with the extended flame of far reaching Mind, measuring all things except that Intelligible. But it is requisite to understand this; for if thou inclinest thy Mind thou wilt understand it, not earnestly; but it is becoming to bring with thee a pure

and enquiring sense, to extend the void mind of thy Soul to the Intelligible, that thou mayest learn the Intelligible, because it subsisteth beyond Mind.

Dam. T.

167. Thou wilt not comprehend it, as when understanding some common thing.

Damascius, *de primis principiis*. T.

168. Ye who understand, know the Super-mundane Paternal Depth.

Dam. Z. or T.

169. Things Divine are not attainable by mortals who understand the body alone, but only by those who stripped of their garments arrive at the summit.

Proc. in *Crat.* Z. or T.

170. Having put on the completely armed-vigour of resounding Light, with triple strength fortifying the Soul and the Mind, He must put into the Mind the various Symbols, and not walk dispersedly on the empyræan path, but with concentration.

171. For being furnished with every kind of Armour, and armed, he is similar to the Goddess.

Proc. in *Pl. Th.*, 324. T.

172. Explore the River of the Soul, whence, or in what order you have come: so that although you have become a servant to the body, you may again rise to the Order from which you descended, joining works to sacred reason.

Psell., 5. *Pletho.* 1. *Z.*

173. Every way unto the emancipated Soul extend the rays of Fire.

Psell., 11. *Pletho*, 24. *Z.*

174. Let the immortal depth of your Soul lead you, but earnestly raise your eyes upwards.

Psell., 11. *Pletho*, 20.

175. Man, being an intelligent Mortal, must bridle his Soul that she may not incur terrestrial infelicity, but be saved.

Lyd., *De Men.*, 2.

176. If thou extendeth the Fiery Mind to the work of piety, thou wilt preserve the fluxible body.

Psell., 22. *Pletho*, 16. *Z.*

177. The telestic life through Divine Fire removeth all the stains, together with everything of a foreign and irrational nature, which the spirit of the Soul has attracted from generation, as we are taught by the Oracle to believe.

Proc. in *Tim.*, 331. Taylor.

178. The Oracles of the Gods declare, that through purifying ceremonies, not the Soul only, but bodies themselves become worthy of receiving much assistance and health, for, say they, the mortal vestment of coarse Matter will by these means be purified." And this, the Gods, in an exhortatory manner, announce to the most holy of Theurgists.

Jul., *Crat.* v., p. 334. Z. or T.

179. We should flee, according to the Oracle, the multitude of men going in a herd.

Proc. in *I. Alc.* Z. or T.

180. Who knoweth himself, knoweth all things in himself.

I. Pic., p. 211. Z.

181. The Oracles often give victory to our own choice, and not to the Order alone of the Mundane periods. As, for instance, when they say, "On beholding thyself, fear!" And again, "Believe thyself to be above the Body, and thou art so." And, still fur-

ther, when they assert, "That our voluntary sorrows germinate in us the growth of the particular life we lead."

Proc., *de Prov.*, p. 483. Z. or T.

182. But these are mysteries which I evolve in the profound Abyss of the Mind.

183. As the Oracle thereforth saith: God is never so turned away from man, and never so much sendeth him new paths, as when he maketh ascent to divine speculation's or works in a confused or disordered manner, and as it adds, with unhallowed lips, or unwashed feet. For of those who are thus negligent, the progress is imperfect, the impulses are vain, and the paths are dark.

Proc. in *Parm.* Z. or T.

184. Not knowing that every God is good, ye are fruitlessly vigilant.

Proc. in *Platonis Pol.*, 355. Z. or T.

185. Theurgists fall not so as to be ranked among the herd that are in subjection to Fate.

Lyd., *De men.* Taylor.

186. The number nine is divine, receives its completion from three triads, and attains the summits of theology, according to the Chaldaic philosophy as Porphyry informeth us.

Lyd.

187. In the left side of Hecate is a fountain of Virtue, which remaineth entirely within her, not sending forth its virginity.

Psell., 13; *Pletho*, 9. Z.

188. And the earth bewailed them, even unto their children.

Psell., 21; *Pletho*, 3. Z.

189. The Furies are the Constrainers of Men.

Psell., 26; *Pletho*, 19. Z.

190. Lest being baptized to the Furies of the Earth, and to the necessities of nature (as some one of the Gods saith), you should perish.

Proc. in *Theol.*, 297. Z. or T.

191. Nature persuadeth us that there are pure Dæmons, and that evil germs of Matter may alike become useful and good.

Psell., 16; *Pletho*, 18. Z.

192. For three days and no longer need ye sacrifice.

Pic. Concl. Z.

193. So therefore first the Priest who governeth the works of Fire, must sprinkle with the Water of the loud-resounding Sea.

Proc. in *Crat.* Z. or T.

194. Labour thou around the Strophalos of Hecaté.

Psell., 9. Nicephorus.

195. When thou shalt see a Terrestrial Dæmon approaching, Cry aloud! and sacrifice the stone Mnizourin.

Psell., 40. Z.

196. If thou often invokest thou shalt see all things growing dark; and then when no longer is visible unto thee the High-arched Vault of Heaven, when the Stars have lost their Light and the Lamp of the Moon is veiled, the Earth abideth not, and around thee darts the Lightning Flame and all things appear amid thunders.

Psell., 10; *Pletho*, 22. Z.

197. From the Cavities of the Earth leap forth the terrestrial Dog-faced demons, showing no true sign unto mortal man.

Psell, 23; *Pletho*, 10. Z.

198. A similar Fire flashingly extending through the rushings of Air, or a Fire formless whence cometh the Image of a Voice, or even a flashing Light abounding, revolving, whirling forth, crying aloud. Also there is the vision of the fire-flashing Courser of Light, or also a Child, borne aloft on the shoulders of the Celestial Steed, fiery, or clothed with gold, or naked, or shooting with the bow shafts of Light, and standing on the shoulders of the horse; then if thy meditation prolongeth itself, thou shalt unite all these Symbols into the Form of a Lion.

Proc. in *Pl. Polit.*, 380; Stanley *Hist. Philos.* Z. or T.

199. When thou shalt behold that holy and formless Fire shining flashingly through the depths of the Universe: Hear thou the Voice of Fire.

Psell., 14; *Pletho*, 25. Z.

ORACLES FROM PORPHYRY

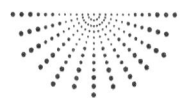

1. There is above the Celestial Lights an Incorruptible Flame always sparkling; the Spring of Life, the Formation of all Beings, the Original of all things! This Flame produceth all things, and nothing perisheth but what it consumeth. It maketh Itself known by Itself. This Fire cannot be contained in any Place, it is without Body and without Matter. It encompasseth the Heavens. And there goeth out from it little Sparks, which make all the Fires of the Sun, of the Moon, and of the Stars. Behold! what I know of God! Strive not to know more of Him, for that is beyond thy capacity, how wise soever thou art. As to the rest, know that unjust and wicked Man cannot hide himself from the Presence of God!

No subtilty nor excuse can disguise anything front His piercing Eyes. All is full of God, and God is in All!

2. There is in God an Immense Profundity of Flame! Nevertheless, the Heart should not fear to approach this Adorable Fire, or to be touched by it; it will never be consumed by this sweet Fire, whose mild and Tranquil Heat maketh the Binding, the Harmony, and the Duration of the World. Nothing subsisteth but by this Fire, which is God Himself. No Person begat Him; He is without Mother; He knoweth all things, and can be taught nothing.

He is Infallible in His designs, and His name is unspeakable, Behold now, what God is! As for us who are His messengers, *We are but a Little Part of God.*

Copyright © 2020 by Alicia Editions
All rights reserved.
Credits: Canva
No part of this book may be reproduced in any form or by any electronic or mechanical means, including information storage and retrieval systems, without written permission from the author, except for the use of brief quotations in a book review.

www.ingramcontent.com/pod-product-compliance
Lightning Source LLC
LaVergne TN
LVHW090037080526
838202LV00046B/3856